This igloo book belongs to:

peter loves teens

igloobooks

Published in 2021
First published in the UK by Igloo Books Ltd
An imprint of Igloo Books Ltd
Cottage Farm, NN6 0BJ, UK
Owned by Bonnier Books
Sveavägen 56, Stockholm, Sweden
www.igloobooks.com

0821 001 PK
4 6 8 10 9 7 5 3
ISBN 978-1-78905-687-7

Written by Gemma Barder
Illustrated by Gabrielle Murphy

Cover designed by Laura Chamberlain

Printed and manufactured in China

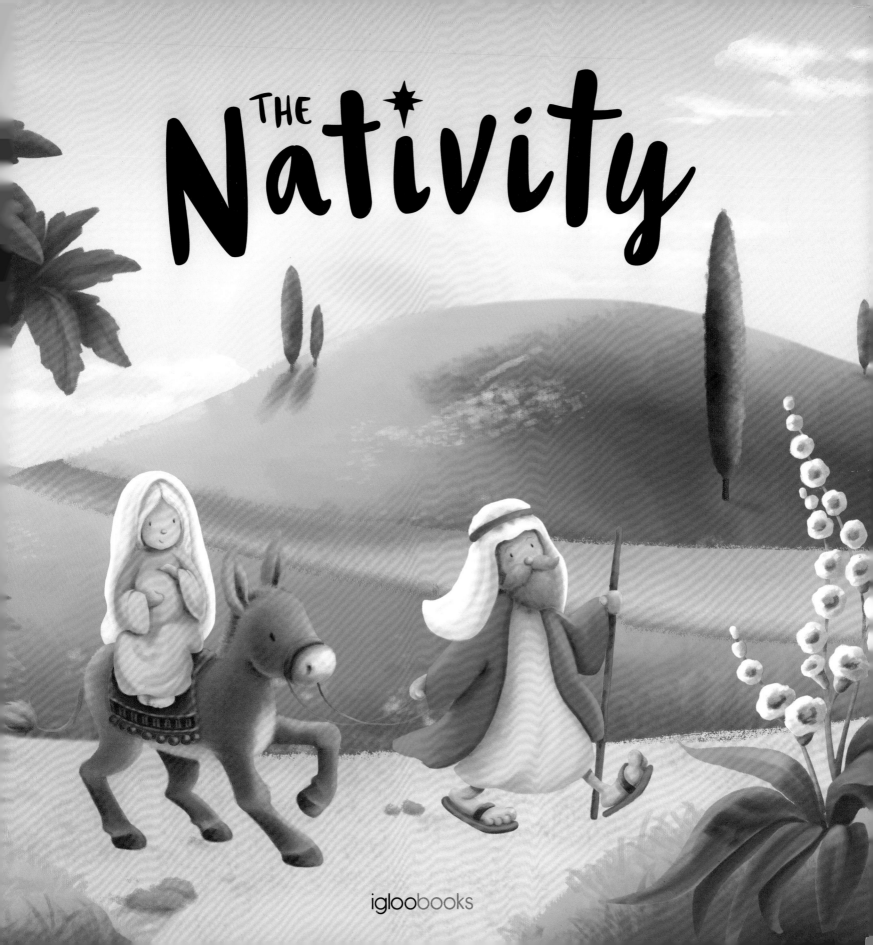

The Nativity

igloobooks

Long ago, in a town called Nazareth, there lived a carpenter named Joseph and his wife, Mary.

Joseph worked all day long in his workshop,
while Mary looked after their little house.

One day, a beautiful, bright light filled Mary and
Joseph's home. It was the Angel Gabriel, who had come
to tell Mary she was going to have a special baby!

Angel Gabriel told Mary that the baby would
be the son of God and that Mary must name him Jesus.

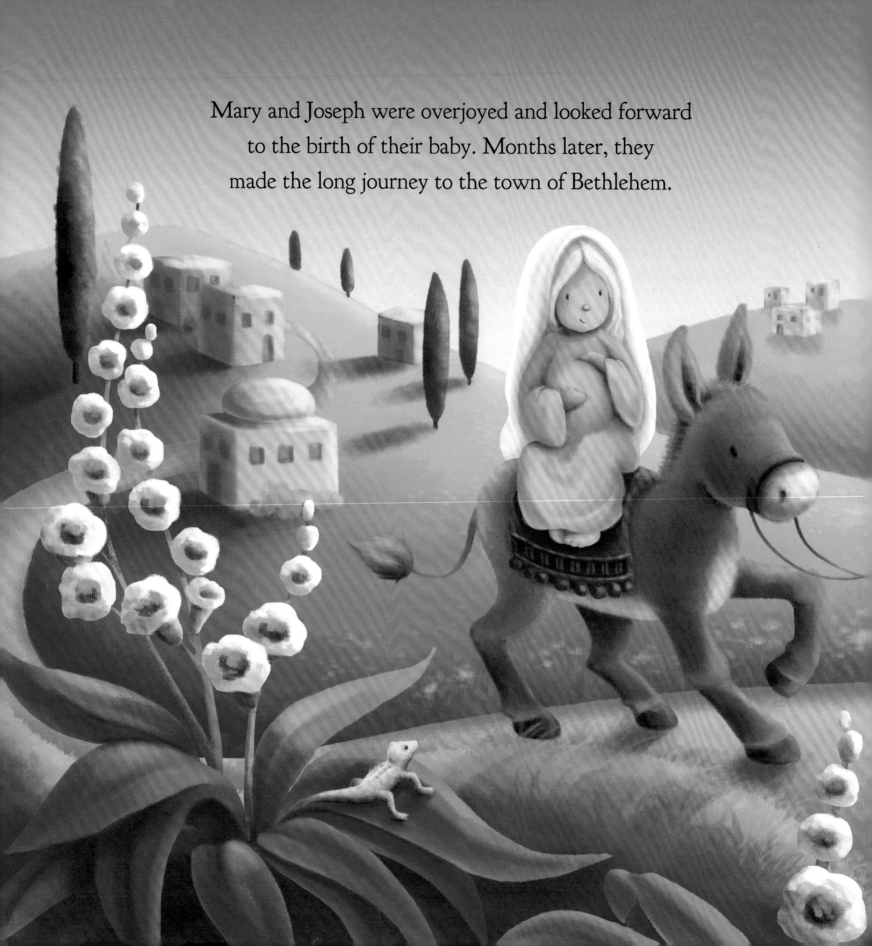

Mary and Joseph were overjoyed and looked forward to the birth of their baby. Months later, they made the long journey to the town of Bethlehem.

They set off over the hills of Galilee, with Mary
riding on the back of a donkey.

When Mary and Joseph arrived in Bethlehem,
they found that there were no rooms left to stay in.

A kind innkeeper saw how tired Mary was
and he offered them his stable for the night.

The stable was warm and dry
and full of friendly animals.
Joseph made a bed of straw
for Mary and they settled
down to sleep.

It was in that stable that Jesus was born.
Mary and Joseph wrapped him in a blanket and
laid him in a manger.

As the animals came to worship Jesus, a bright
star settled over the stable.

High on the hills outside Bethlehem, three shepherds
were watching their flock. Suddenly, an angel
appeared in the sky.

"Do not be afraid," the angel said.
"The son of God has been born!"

Far away, in the East, three wise men
saw the bright star shining in the sky.

They had read in ancient scrolls that when a new
star appeared, it meant there was a great new king.

The wise men journeyed all through the night,
following the star across the desert.

It led them to the stable in Bethlehem
where Jesus had been born.

The wise men gave Jesus gifts of gold, frankincense
and myrrh, while the shepherds promised to spread
the word of Jesus' birth far and wide.

They all worshipped, for the
son of God was born!